Peace on the Playground

PEACE ON THE PLAYGROUND

Nonviolent Ways of Problem-Solving

by Eileen Lucas

A FIRST BOOK
FRANKLIN WATTS
NEW YORK/LONDON/TORONTO/SYDNEY
1991

Also by Eileen Lucas

Vincent Van Gogh

Cover photograph copyright ©: Photo Researchers, Inc.

Photographs copyright ©: Impact Visuals: pp. 8 (Kirk Condyles), 17 (Graeme Williams), 26 (Robert Fox), 40 (Ricky Flores), 41 (T.L. Litt); UPI/Bettmann Newsphotos: pp. 13, 14; Ellen B. Senisi: p. 18; R. Bruce Thompson: pp. 21, 28, 30, 37, 49, 52; Steven Borns: p. 25; Randy Matusow: p. 32; Wide World Photos: pp. 38, 44; Gamma-Liaison: pp. 35 (Steve Schapiro), 45 (John Chaisson); Janet Wojcik: p. 50.

Library of Congress Cataloging-in-Publication Data

Lucas, Eileen.
    Peace on the playground : nonviolent ways of problem-solving / by
Eileen Lucas.
        p.   cm. — (A First book)
    Includes bibliographical references and index.
    Summary: Introduces the concept of nonviolent resolution of
conflicts. Includes practical tips, hands-on activities, and
appropriate role models for guidance and inspiration.
    ISBN 0-531-20047-7
    1. Nonviolence—Juvenile literature.   2. Conflict management—
Juvenile literature.   3. Peace—Juvenile literature.
[1. Nonviolence. 2. Conflict management.] I. Title. II. Series.
HM278.L83   1991
303.6′9—dc20   91-12099   CIP   AC

Contents

For my children, Travis and Brendan, and for all
our children, that they may reach peace

My thanks to Bruce and Joan Thompson,
Ben Thompson, Bill Anderson, Johanna Anderson,
Caleb Ritter, Chandelle Black, David Hohisel,
Dennis Hohisel, Derrick Hohisel, Travis Lucas,
and Janet Wojcik. Special thanks to Linda
Lantieri, coordinator for the Resolving Conflict
Creatively Program of New York City,
for reviewing the manuscript.

Children around the world are
marching for peace.

Introduction

What does the word "peace" mean to you? When asked this question, one child responded, "Peace is people talking together with a heart in between them."[1]

Talking—communicating—certainly seems to be an important part of peace. It is mentioned many times when people are asked what peace means to them.

What does peace mean to you? Take a minute to think about it. Do you think peace is possible? In your family or neighborhood? Between the nations of our world?

One eleven-year-old said, "Peace to me is that apple that is high on a branch on your tree—it's just out of your reach. Yet if we want it bad enough, we will make that extra effort to go in the garage and get a ladder."[2]

That's what this book is all about. It is time for everyone to get up and find a ladder. It's time for everyone to take a bite out of the apple of peace. One of the ways we can make this happen is by learning to solve our everyday problems peacefully. The following chapters will discuss the concept of nonviolent conflict resolution—solving problems without causing harm to others. From problems between two friends to problems between nations, nonviolent conflict resolution is a tool people everywhere can use to make this a more peaceful world to live in. It can be the ladder we use to reach peace.

Peace in Action 1

You probably know a lot more about war than you do about peace. The causes and effects of war are studied in school. We read about generals and the outcome of battles. But the subject of peace is often ignored.

There is a lot to learn about peace and the special techniques of peace known as *nonviolence*. Nonviolence, which means that people try to find solutions to problems without harming others, has been around for a long, long time. Examples of nonviolence can be found as far back as ancient times. Sometimes religious and political leaders have tried to teach their followers the ways of peace. More often, it has been the work of common citizens to try to teach their leaders to abandon the ways of war.

Individuals who have stood up and said that fighting was wrong when everyone else around them was turning to violence have had to be very brave and strong in spirit. Even though some people think that anyone who won't fight is a coward, history has shown that choosing nonviolence is truly a hero's choice.

These champions of peace have come from all races and nationalities. They have been men, women, and even children. They have risked their reputations, their jobs, and even their lives in choosing peace. They've actually had to fight, and fight hard, for what they believed in, but they used weapons of nonviolence—such as talking, *negotiating*, and *boycotting*—instead of weapons of violence, such as fists and guns.

An example of a leader who was both a *nonviolent activist* and a *pacifist* was Mohandas (Mahatma) Gandhi. In 1906 he helped Indians who were living in South Africa fight a group of unfair laws, using nonviolent techniques. Later he used these same techniques in India to lead the Indian people in their fight for freedom. The teachings of Gandhi about nonviolence have become famous all over the world and have inspired many other people to use the same means for resolving conflicts.

One of the most famous examples was a young black preacher named Martin Luther King Jr. Dr. King applied the methods of nonviolence in the fight

Mohandas (Mahatma) Gandhi believed
that nonviolent action was a better way
to solve problems than violent action.
He spent most of his adult life
promoting the use of nonviolence.

against *segregation* and *prejudice* in the South of the United States. He also used nonviolence to fight *injustice* in the big cities of the North. This fight against injustice in the 1960s was known as the Civil Rights movement.

As one of the leaders of this movement, Dr. King stressed again and again the importance of nonviolence in creating change. He believed in the power of love. He even went so far as to love his enemies. "The nonviolent resister not only refuses to shoot his opponent," he said, "but he also refuses to hate him."[1]

These are just a couple of examples of the many times throughout history when people have chosen nonviolence and peace instead of violence and war. Sometimes the decision has been successful, sometimes not. But in each case, peacemakers have refused to use violence to solve their problems.

Dr. Martin Luther King Jr. promoted the use of nonviolence in the struggle for equality and justice for all people.

Violence and Conflict 2

Violence is probably something you're very aware of. Maybe you've been the victim of violent actions yourself or know someone else who has been. Surely you've seen violence on television and heard about it on the radio.

Violence is not the same as conflict. A *conflict* is a problem, a difference, between two persons or groups of persons. Conflict is normal and is always going to be around because the world is full of differences.

Conflict is not necessarily bad. Sometimes it results in growth and changes for the better. Problems with conflict develop when we are not good at handling it.

When people find themselves in a conflict situation, they tend to think of violence as the only way out. But there are *always* nonviolent choices in any situation as well. When you choose a nonviolent way

This child is growing up in
a place where violence
threatens his life
every day . . .

. . . but all of us have to deal
with conflict in some form.

to deal with a problem, you are trying to find a solution that will avoid harming others. If you choose to use violence, you are choosing to hurt someone.

There are many kinds of violence. Physical violence is what we usually think of first—hurting someone's body or belongings in some way. But verbal and emotional abuse are violence as well. The inner wounds caused by such acts as teasing, ignoring, or yelling at people can be just as painful as the outer wounds of physical violence.

A common form of everyday violence occurs when we label people with words that put them down—words like "nerds" and "weirdos." By calling people names, we are telling ourselves that somehow the other person doesn't count as much as we do. Maybe we are trying to make ourselves feel better, but doing this at someone else's expense simply isn't fair.

When we watch a movie, we want the good guys to win, and often we don't care how they go about it. Violence committed by the bad guys, we say, is wrong; but the same act performed by the good guys draws our applause. Why?

Now think about the way you usually deal with conflicts. Can you think of any better ways to handle them, ways that might allow everyone involved to feel like a winner? The next chapter may help you solve this problem.

Peace on the Playground 3

Think about how you usually handle conflict situations. Let's say someone has just called you a name, or knocked down your bike, or thrown something at you. You're angry. What do you do?

Most likely you want to fight back. That person has hurt you in some way and now you want to hurt him or her in return. But what will be the result of that? Will it make the person sorry about what has been done?

Probably not. Probably it will only make the person want to hurt you even more. This is what is known as a vicious circle. A violent act usually results in a violent response, which in turn tends to cause even more violence.

But what if you don't respond with a violent act? Can we learn to stop the vicious circle before it gets rolling?

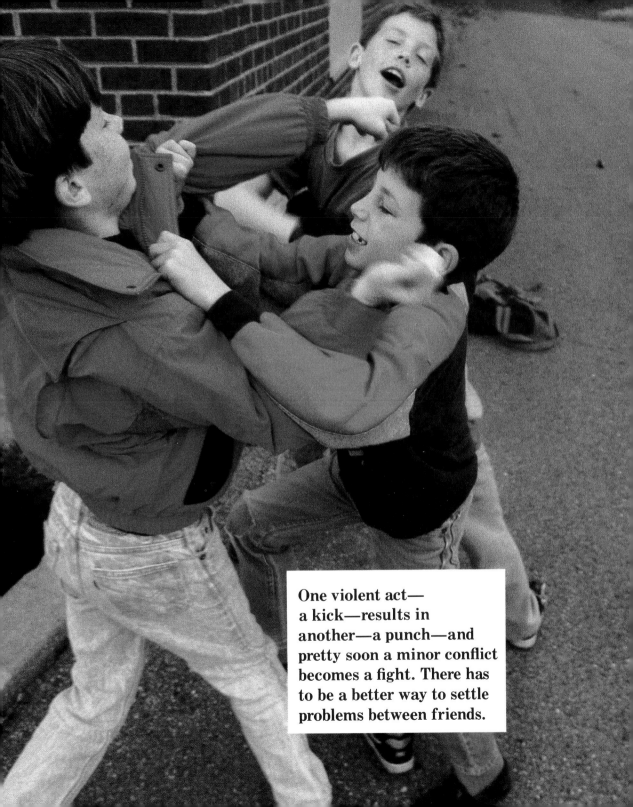

One violent act—
a kick—results in
another—a punch—and
pretty soon a minor conflict
becomes a fight. There has
to be a better way to settle
problems between friends.

Yes, we can. And that's what this chapter is all about. When confronted with a violent act, we need to stop and make some choices about how to respond. The following chart shows that between the choices of doing nothing, and fighting, are a whole group of other possible actions we call nonviolent responses.

Conflict Situation

Choices

to do nothing   to act violently

to act

nonviolently

negotiate   listening   letter-writing campaign. . . . → boycott

It is important to note that choosing nonviolence doesn't mean that you can't be angry. When someone does something that hurts you, it's normal to be angry. It's what you choose to do with that anger that conflict-solving is all about. Sometimes you may choose to do nothing. There may be times when the best way to handle a situation is to walk away from it until you are better prepared to deal with it.

But most of the time you will probably want to do

something. Rather than acting in a violent way, such as yelling or hitting, you can express your anger in a nonviolent way, such as explaining how you feel, asking for information, or seeking the help of a third person.

What kinds of things can you do to solve a problem without violence? The following are a few ideas, not all of which apply to every situation. Every conflict is different, so you will have to think about which actions will work best in your situation. There is no one right answer that will work every time.

Nonviolent Responses to Conflict

1. Talk about the problem. You can try to explain something that the other person might not have understood or give the person information that might change his or her mind about the situation. Negotiation, which is a special kind of communication between two or more people, is an effective way to talk out a conflict.

2. Be a good listener. This means more than just hearing the words the other person is saying. Let the other person know you are really interested in what's being said. It makes that person feel better and helps make a solution easier to find.

3. Ask someone who's not involved to help. This is called seeking the help of a third party. Sometimes

someone who is not personally involved in the conflict can help the people involved find a fair solution that they might not have thought of otherwise. This person is called a *mediator*.

4. Get more people involved. When the conflict involves trying to get something changed, you might be more successful if you get lots of people to help. Some of the ways to do this include public speeches, petitions, *letter-writing campaigns*, and *picketing*.

5. Drama, music, and stories. Putting on plays, singing songs, and writing stories that convey your message can be a dramatic way of getting your point across.

6. Public acts draw attention to your cause. Again, this works well when you are trying to achieve change in a nonviolent way. Public acts can range from displaying posters or wearing certain items of clothing to parades, marches, and *sit-ins*.

7. Boycotts and strikes. These involve refusing to buy from or work for persons with whom you have a conflict. Boycotts and strikes can be very powerful tools, and they should be used very carefully and only when other efforts haven't worked.

8. Agree to disagree. In some cases, maybe you can decide that you each can respect the other's position and leave it at that.

When a third party gets involved—whether
it's a young person or an adult—he or she can
sometimes help the people in conflict reach a
peaceful, creative solution.

Bringing a problem to the attention of a large
group of people is a good way to enlist the help
of other concerned individuals. These children
traveled all the way from El Salvador to
New York to demonstrate their need for help.

These are just some of the ways problems can be worked out nonviolently. The first three options listed are the most commonly used ways of solving conflicts peacefully. The others are generally used in more serious conflict situations involving large numbers of people.

How do you decide how to go about solving a conflict you are involved in? One way is to follow a problem-solving plan, which goes something like this:

1. Define the problem so that everyone agrees on exactly what it is.
2. Think up as many possible solutions to the problem as you can, accepting all ideas without criticism. This is called *brainstorming*, and is a very important part of creative conflict-solving.
3. Discuss the various possibilities, perhaps combining or eliminating some.
4. Narrow down the choices, trying to arrive at the best possible solution.
5. Decide how to put the solution into action.
6. Be prepared to evaluate how well the solution is working and be open to trying something else, if needed.

Part of learning to solve problems peacefully is changing your attitude of always wanting to be "the

Brainstorming, in which everyone
thinks up as many solutions as
possible, can be very effective
in problem-solving.

winner." You don't always have to face conflicts as a question of "me against you and one of us must lose." Instead, you can think in terms of "you and me working together" to find a solution.

One technique for learning this way of thinking is to practice playing cooperative games. Some people describe cooperative games as games without winners. Another way to think of them is as games without losers. These are sometimes called win/win games, because the way for you to win is by helping other people win too.

At first you might think that playing a game in which the object is something other than winning might not be much fun. But if winning means defeating someone, that someone might not be having as much fun as you. Thus, in cooperative games, more people can actually have fun.

Cooperative games teach us to enjoy games for their own sake, for the sake of friendship, and sometimes for the sheer fun of physical activity. In this way, all who participate are winners, and that's what we should strive for in conflict-solving, too. The more we learn to work together with people (rather than trying to defeat them), the easier it will be to solve problems creatively and peacefully.

An example of a cooperative game that you're probably already familiar with is Frisbee.® The ob-

Learning to play games in a cooperative manner
(me *and* you, rather than me *against* you) is a big
step toward learning creative conflict-solving.

ject of this game is to enjoy yourself, and anyone who does, wins.

Almost any game you play with someone else can be a cooperative game if you have the right attitude. Building something with a friend, either with blocks, other building toys, or with real tools and materials, can be a cooperative and rewarding play experience. Even competitive games like basketball and checkers can be played with a cooperative attitude. Don't make winning or losing the main objective. Treat the game as a learning experience, or as a chance to share a friend's company. You'll be enjoying yourself—as well as practicing a conflict-solving skill.

One of the keys to nonviolent conflict-solving is learning to confront people with whom you disagree without attacking them, physically or verbally. Keep your energy focused on fighting the problem, not each other. Try not to get distracted into name-calling or other such behavior.

If someone else starts to use name-calling, you can try to get things back on track by using "I" messages. For example, you might say something like, "I feel bad when you make fun of the way I speak, and I don't think it's going to help us solve this problem. I'm doing the best I can and I'd really like to try to work this out."

Of course, all this is easier said than done. But like anything else worthwhile, the more you practice it, the easier it will become. Start with a fairly small conflict at home or at school and try some of these problem-solving tips. Don't be discouraged if they don't work right away. Even people who have studied conflict resolution for years still have trouble solving some of their problems. It isn't easy. But if you keep trying and keep yourself open to the other person's point of view, it will start to pay off. Your new behavior will help you to avoid some conflicts, and it will make others easier to handle. That will make it all worthwhile.

Even a game with only two players, such as checkers, can be played with a cooperative spirit. It is more important to concentrate on how well you play than on whether or not you win.

Peace on the Planet   4

What about conflicts between nations? Is there anything that we as individuals can do about that?

Yes, there is. After all, nations are made up of individuals just like you and me. If more and more people in any particular nation would practice non-violent problem-solving in their own lives, they would send a clear message to their leaders. When violence becomes an unpopular choice among the people of a nation, it is less likely to be popular among its leaders as well.

And when the citizens of a country are peacefully working out problems among themselves, they will be better at reaching out to the citizens of other countries.

Many people around the world are already doing this. They are called *citizen diplomats*. Citizen diplo-

People can learn to live in harmony
when similarities are appreciated
and differences are respected.

mats are people of all ages and backgrounds who understand that if the people of the world can get along, it will be easier for their governments to get along as well.

Citizen diplomats believe that anything an individual can do to promote understanding among people helps to promote peace. A simple thing such as having a pen pal from another country, contributing to an international hunger organization, or hosting a foreign exchange student can emphasize that all the people of the world are just that—people. And people working together to solve problems is what peace and peaceful conflict-solving are all about.

One girl who showed us that the more we learn about each other, the easier it is to live in peace, was Samantha Smith of Manchester, Maine. When Samantha was ten years old, she wrote a letter to the Russian leader Yuri Andropov, asking him why the Russians wanted war with the United States. A few months later, Samantha received a personal response from Mr. Andropov, explaining that the Soviet people wanted peace as well. He invited Samantha and her parents to visit the Soviet Union. The Smiths accepted the invitation, and during the trip, Samantha met many Soviet children. She discovered that they cared about peace and friendship, just as she did.

Over the next few years, Samantha traveled

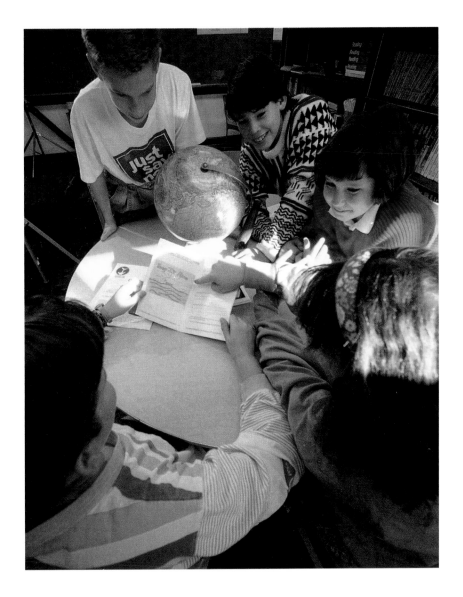

Anything that contributes to international
understanding contributes to peace.

Samantha Smith (second from right) taught us
all that getting to know people from other countries
helps break down barriers that lead to conflict.

around the United States and to several other countries, telling people about her experience. Then, in August 1985, Samantha and her father died in a plane crash. People all over the world were saddened at her death.

It is important to remember that Samantha Smith *did* something. She did not worry about solving all the world's problems overnight, but just did what she could do. She wrote a letter. And then she was not afraid to talk to people about it, to discuss her hopes and fears, to honestly describe her impressions and thoughts.

While finding out about the things we have in common with each other is one way to bring people closer together, this doesn't mean that we all must be alike. In many ways, various groups of people *are* different, and that's one of the things that makes life interesting. "Share our similarities, celebrate our differences,"[1] says author Scott Peck. He's trying to tell us that we need to be more accepting of the ways in which each of us is different.

It's a little like the concept of harmony in music, where unique and different notes work together, complementing one another. We don't all have to sing the same notes all the time. A song will be richer for all the different voices and notes joining together. We just have to sing notes that do not spoil the notes of

Nelson and Winnie Mandela (left) and
Archbishop Desmond Tutu (above) have
spoken out bravely in their country and
around the world in favor of equality and
justice in their native South Africa.

others. Interdependent does not mean "the same." It means working together even though the individual parts might be different.

Dr. Martin Luther King Jr., who saw a connection between many of the world's greatest problems—racial injustice, poverty, and war—once said that he spoke "as a citizen of the world." As citizens of the world, each of us needs to do what he or she can to make the world a better place for all its people.

Peace Is Possible 5

There is no guarantee that nonviolent methods of problem-solving will work in every case. But violence is not guaranteed either, and there are always some positive results to acting in a peaceful way.

One very positive outcome of learning nonviolent techniques is that people realize that there is something they can do about problems that might otherwise seem beyond their control. For example, during the Civil Rights movement, many of the black people in the South found out that there were things they could do to try to change the injustices they had been facing for generations. Maybe they couldn't eliminate all the injustices and all the hate at once, but they could start to try to make things better.

The ability to feel good about yourself and what you're doing is another benefit of learning about non-

(Above) Peace starts with solving
everyday problems creatively
and nonviolently.

(Left) Promoters of nonviolence believe
that this is the right way to achieve change.
Civil rights demonstrators like these
marchers in the 1960s used nonviolent
means to promote their cause.

violence. Setting aside fear and hate, and feeling good about who you are, is a positive result in and of itself. And the more people learn about and practice the techniques of nonviolence, the more likely it is they will become successful at using them.

But even when nonviolent methods do not succeed in problem-solving, promoters of nonviolence say that they will continue to choose them if for no other reason than it is the moral way of handling disagreements. For many peacemakers, this is the most important thing about nonviolence: it is a better way to solve problems. This belief helps them to continue to work for peaceful solutions even in the midst of violence, because "success" is not the reason they became involved in the first place.

One peacemaker explained it this way: "I believe in peace, even though it seems like a dream. I would rather chase a jackrabbit all over Iowa and not catch him than chase a skunk halfway around the block and catch him. I would rather go for the dream of peace and fail than go for the skunk of war, hatred and bloodshed and succeed."[1]

The dream of peace will be possible when we start solving our problems, one at a time, without violence. When there is peace on the playground and peace in our neighborhoods, we will be that much closer to peace on the planet Earth.

Becoming a   6
Peacemaker

Learning to solve conflicts peacefully is an ongoing process. You can't just read about it once and then expect to be good at it. You have to keep adding to what you know and keep reminding yourself to use what you have learned.

Books

One of the best ways to learn more is to read as much as you can about peace and peacemakers. At the end of this book is a list of books you can read "For Further Reading." Your school or public librarian can help you find these and other good books.

In addition, there are many excellent biographies of peacemakers. Learning how other people have applied the concepts of peace to their lives is very helpful if you want to become a peacemaker yourself. Some of these people include: Jane Addams, Sequoya, Benjamin Franklin, Mahatma Gandhi, Eleanor Roosevelt, Albert Schweitzer, Martin Luther King Jr., Mother Theresa, Desmond Tutu, and many, many others.

Clubs

A good way to practice peacemaking skills is by forming a peace club. An organization called Children As the Peacemakers has some information you can send for that will tell you how you can be part of an official peace group. It would help to have an adult who would work with your club and act as a guide. The group's address is:

Children As the Peacemakers
Peace Clubs
950 Battery St., Second Floor
San Francisco, California 94111

You can also start a less formal peace club on your own with a group of your friends. Club meetings would be a good time to practice some of the things you've learned here and in other books about peace and nonviolence. It would be good to keep membership open to anyone who wants to participate in peacemaking efforts.

Forming a club with other people
who care about peace is a good way
to put what you've learned about
peacemaking into action.

The cast of this performance of the play
Peace Child was made up of young people from
Illinois, Wisconsin, and the Soviet Union.

Some of the things that your peace club could sponsor might include doing errands or chores for elderly or sick neighbors, cleaning up a vacant lot or other dirty place, having a bake sale or other money-raising activity for a good cause, and putting on plays or concerts to generate positive feelings in your community. There are many more ideas. Remember, anything you do to create good feelings between people or to make the world a better place is peacemaking!

Plays

Ask the appropriate teacher at your school if you can put on the Peace Child play. This play has been performed by students all over the country and has helped many young people (and adults too!) to think about Soviet citizens in a different light. It's a great junior high school project, but could be adapted for younger students as well. The address to write to is:

Peace Child Foundation
3977 Chain Bridge Rd., Suite 204
Fairfax, Virginia 22030

You could also make up your own play about what peace means to you, or about how people can work problems out without violence.

Having a foreign pen pal is a good way to increase your understanding of what it is like to live in another country.

Pen Pals

Finding a pen pal in a foreign country is a fine way to develop international understanding. The more we know about the people of other countries, the easier it will be to get along. Here are some addresses to contact to find out how to get an international pen pal. (You might also check with your school to find out if there are any students who come from another country. They might be able to help you find a pen pal in that country, and you might even gain a new friend at the same time!)

Kids Meeting Kids
  Can Make a Difference
Box 8H, 380 Riverside Dr.
New York, New York 10025

Letters for Peace
238 Autumn Ridge Rd.
Fairfield, Connecticut 06432

Samantha Smith Center
9 Union St.
Hallowell, Maine 04340

World Pen Pals
World Affairs Center
University of Minnesota
Minneapolis, Minnesota 55455

Glossary

Boycott—to stay away from or avoid buying something as a way of showing displeasure

Brainstorming—letting your imagination go so you can think up as many ideas as possible

Citizen diplomats—people from around the world who work for international peace by reaching out to people from other countries

Conflict—a difference between two or more people that is a problem for at least one of them

Injustice—something that is not right or fair

Letter-writing campaign—lots of people write letters to a particular person or organization, letting them know how they feel about something

Mediator—a "third person" who is not directly involved in a conflict, whose job it is to help the persons in conflict reach a solution

Negotiation—communication between two or more people for the purpose of settling a conflict in a way that is fair to all sides

Nonviolence—that which does not cause harm to others

Nonviolent activist—someone who acts in nonviolent ways to achieve a certain goal

Pacifist—someone who believes that violence is wrong under any circumstances and refuses to participate in it

Picketing—standing outside a building, often carrying posters or signs, as a way of protesting something going on inside the building

Prejudice—prejudging; thinking you know all about someone, especially in a negative way, based on one or two outward characteristics. Being prejudiced means lumping people together into categories, forgetting that each person is a unique blend of many factors.

Segregation—restricted or separated by group or race

Sit-in—when people sit down in a particular place in protest of something

Source Notes

Introduction
1. Jampolsky, Gerald G., M.D., ed., *Children as Teachers of Peace*, Celestial Arts, Berkeley, Calif., 1982, p. 30.
2. Ibid., p. 38.

Chapter One
1. Sharp, Gene, *The Politics of Nonviolent Action*, Porter Sargent Publishers, Boston, 1973, p. 635.

Chapter Four
1. Peck, M. Scott, *The Different Drum*, Simon and Schuster, New York, 1987.

Chapter Five
1. Arnett, Ronald C., *Dwell in Peace*, The Brethren Press, Elgin, Illinois, 1980, p. 47.

Bibliography

Bickmore, Kathy. *Alternatives to Violence.* Akron, Ohio: Peace Grows, Inc., 1987.

Boston Area Educators for Social Responsibility. *Perspectives, A Teaching Guide to Concepts of Peace.* Cambridge, Massachusetts, 1983.

Challinor, Joan, and Robert Beisner, eds. *Arms at Rest: Peace-making and Peacekeeping in American History.* Westport, Connecticut: Greenwood Press, 1987.

Dorn, Lois. *Peace in the Family.* New York: Pantheon Books, 1983.

Fisher, Roger and William Ury. *Getting to Yes: Negotiating Agreement Without Giving In.* Boston: Houghton Mifflin, 1981.

Schmidt, Fran, and Alice Friedman. *Creative Conflict Solving for Kids.* Miami Beach: Peace Education Foundation, 1985.

Warner, Gale, and Michael Shuman. *Citizen Diplomats.* New York: Continuum Publishing Co., 1987.

For Further Reading

Aaseng, Nathen. *The Peace Seekers: The Nobel Peace Prize*. Minneapolis: Lerner Publications, 1987.

Durell, Ann, and Marilyn Sachs. *The Big Book for Peace*. New York: E. P. Dutton, 1990.

Galichich, Anne. *Samantha Smith: A Journey for Peace*. Minneapolis: Dillon, 1987.

Jampolsky, Gerald G. *Children as Teachers of Peace*. Berkeley: Celestial Arts, 1986.

Lowery, Linda. *Martin Luther King Day*. Minneapolis: Carolrhoda Books, 1987.

MacDonald, Fiona. *Working for Equality*. New York: Franklin Watts, 1988.

Meltzer, Milton. *Ain't Gonna Study War No More: The Story of America's Peace Seekers*. New York: Harper & Row, 1985.

Index

Page numbers in *italics* refer to illustrations.